Problem Solving Made Easy

AGES 7–9

Author and Consultant
Sean McArdle

Certificate

Congratulations to

....
(write your name here)

for successfully finishing this book.

GOOD JOB!

You're a star.

AGES 7–9

Key Stage 2

Date

....

DK | Penguin Random House

DK London
Editors Elizabeth Blakemore, Jolyon Goddard
Senior Art Editor Ann Cannings
Managing Editor Christine Stroyan
Managing Art Editor Anna Hall
Senior Production Editor Andy Hilliard
Senior Production Controller Jude Crozier
Jacket Design Development Manager Sophia MTT
Publisher Andrew Macintyre
Associate Publishing Director Liz Wheeler
Art Director Karen Self
Publishing Director Jonathan Metcalf

DK Delhi
Senior Editor Rupa Rao
Editor Arpita Nath
Art Editors Baibhav Parida, Yamini Panwar, Tanvi Nathyal
Managing Editors Soma B. Chowdhury, Kingshuk Ghoshal
Managing Art Editors Ahlawat Gunjan, Govind Mittal
DTP Designers Anita Yadav, Rakesh Kumar, Harish Aggarwal
Senior Jacket Designer Suhita Dharamjit
Jackets Editorial Coordinator Priyanka Sharma

This edition published in 2020
First published in Great Britain in 2016 by
Dorling Kindersley Limited
DK, One Embassy Gardens, 8 Viaduct Gardens, London, SW11 7BW

A CIP catalogue record for this book is available from the British Library.
ISBN 978-0-2412-2498-4

Printed and bound in Great Britain by Bell and Bain Ltd, Glasgow

For the curious

www.dk.com

Contents

This chart lists all the topics in the book. When you have completed each page, colour in a star in the correct box. When you have finished the book, sign and date the certificate.

Bobby spent £14 when he went out on Saturday afternoon. He spent £3.20 on his bus fare, £8.50 on magazines and the rest on snacks. How much did Bobby spend on snacks?

$$3.20 + 8.50 = 11.70$$

$$\begin{array}{r} 14.00 \\ -\ 11.70 \\ \hline 02.30 \end{array}$$

£2.30

Jane spent £4.60 on a birthday present for her mother. She also bought a card and wrapping paper, which cost her an additional £2.80. How much did Jane spend in total?

Jason and Vicky have collected a total of 187 football cards for their football album. If Jason collected 92 cards, how many cards did Vicky collect for the album?

cards

Last month, Jared earned £20. In the same month, however, he bought a book for £4 and a shirt for £11. Did Jared manage to save any money that month? If so, how much?

....

The total of three numbers is 124. If two of the numbers are 30 and 55, what is the third number?

Margo added up the money she was given on her birthday and found she had exactly £21. Her aunt gave her £10, her sister gave her £2.50 and her uncle gave her the rest. How much money did Margo's uncle give her?

Ian organised an anniversary party for his parents. He sent out 84 invites, but only 67 people confirmed. On the day of the party, however, 7 more of those who were invited turned up. How many invited people did not attend the party?

$67 + 7 = 74$

$$\begin{array}{r} 84 \\ -74 \\ \hline 10 \end{array}$$

[10] people

In a class of 31 children, 8 have blue eyes, 19 have brown eyes and the rest have green eyes. How many children in the class have green eyes?

[ ] children

A delivery van driver wanted to find out how many kilometres he travelled last week. He made a note of all the distances he had driven that week. They were 31 km, 63 km, 48 km, 90 km and 53 km. How many kilometres had he travelled in total?

[ ]

Louise downloaded three songs from the internet. Two of the downloads cost 79 p each and the third cost 99 p. How much did Louise pay altogether? Give your answer in pounds and pence.

[ ]

When Sonia subtracted a number she had chosen from 150, the result was 89. Which number did Sonia choose?

[ ]

When Sean checked the receipt for his shopping, he noticed that he had spent £57.80 on groceries and the rest on cleaning products. If the total on the receipt was £85, how much did Sean spend on cleaning products?

[ ]

★ Times tables 1

What is two times two times two?	$2 \times 2 = 4$
8	$4 \times 2 = 8$

If four eights are 32, what will eight eights be?

[   ]

How many days are the same as eight weeks?

[   ] days

If 12 fours are 48, what will six fours be?

[   ]

Double four and then double it again. What is the answer?

[   ]

Emily halves a number and the result is 16.
What was the original number that she chose?

[   ]

When five is multiplied by a mystery number,
the answer is 60. What is the mystery number?

[   ]

If 12 times 12 is 144, what will six times 12 be?

[   ]

Which number when multiplied by itself gives 121?	11 x 11 = 121
11	

Which number gives the answer 56 when multiplied by eight?

Which number gives the answer 56 when multiplied by eight?

How many months are the same as five years?

months

Last month, 11 people in Amy's office contributed £10 each to a charity. What was the total amount of money raised by the office workers?

To keep fit, Simon walks 5 km each day. If he has already completed 40 km, how many days has Simon been going for walks?

days

Write the answers to these questions as quickly as you can.

6 x 7 =   9 x 3 =   10 x 12 =   7 x 7 =

What is the missing number in each sum?

5 x   = 25   x 8 = 40   7 x   = 21   x 12 = 24

An art teacher gives each child in his class three types of paintbrush. If there are eight children in the class, how many paintbrushes will he need in total?

paintbrushes

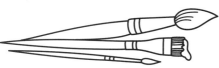

Mr Brydon spent all Sunday making muffins for a school cake sale. He packed the muffins six to a box and filled 12 boxes. How many muffins did Mr Brydon have altogether?

| 72 | muffins

$$\begin{array}{r} 12 \\ \times\ 6 \\ \hline 72 \end{array}$$

To brighten up her garden in spring, Marie planted tulip bulbs. She made three rows in the flower bed and planted 12 bulbs in each row. How many bulbs in all did Marie plant?

| | tulip bulbs

Marcel divided his postcard collection equally among his five nieces and nephews. If Marcel had a collection of 150 postcards, how many did each child receive?

| | postcards

Ben gave each guest at his party eight mini burgers. Nine guests came to his party. How many burgers did Ben need for his guests?

| | burgers

If 60 library books need to be put in piles of 12, how many piles will there be?

| | piles

A number multiplied by seven is 63. What is the number?

| |

Each text message Jada sends costs her 6 p. If Jada sent 40 messages last month, how much did it cost her? Give your answer in pounds and pence.

| |

Lee bought six box sets of books for his nephew. If one box set contains five books, how many books did Lee buy?

5
x   6
30

[30] books

How many years are the same as nine decades?

[   ] years

Daniel had 19 cupcakes. He gave four of his friends four cupcakes each. How many cupcakes were then left for Daniel to eat?

[   ] cupcakes

A hotel's chef used 84 eggs to make breakfast for the hotel's guests this morning. If each egg box holds a dozen eggs, how many boxes did he use?

[   ] egg boxes

Which number multiplied by three gives the answer 66?

[   ]

If a potter takes 20 minutes to make one eggcup, how many eggcups can she make in four hours?

[   ] eggcups

If a packet of biscuits contains 24 biscuits, how many biscuits will be there in four packets?

[   ] biscuits

★ Time problems 1

For breakfast, Dan likes to boil his eggs for four-and-a-half minutes. How long is that in seconds?

| 270 seconds |

1 minute = 60 seconds

$4 \times 60 = 240$

$\frac{1}{2}$ minute = 30 seconds

$$\begin{array}{r} 240 \\ + 30 \\ \hline 270 \end{array}$$

Emma went shopping at 10.00 a.m. and returned at 2.30 p.m. How long did Emma shop for? Give your answer in hours and minutes.

Harris likes to tell his age in months instead of years. If Harris is six-and-a-half years old, how would he say his age?

months

George has been alive for five-and-a-half decades. How old is George in years?

years

Which two months in a row have 31 days?

....

While swimming, David managed to do the front crawl for 11 seconds, while Taylor managed to do it for 20 seconds. How much longer than David did Taylor manage to do the crawl?

It took Elizabeth 35 minutes to walk to Winchester's city centre from her home. If Elizabeth left her home at 8.45 a.m., what time did she reach the city centre?

Carmen has not yet learned the 24-hour system for telling the time. She sees that it is 20:00, but doesn't understand what time that is. Can you help her?

| 8.00 p.m. |

For times later than 12:00 (noon), take away 12 hours to give you the p.m. time.

20 – 12 = 8

Olga had to meet her mother at the farmers' market at 14:00. Is that time in the morning or the afternoon?

....

Bartek played in a football match that started at 3.30 p.m. What time was that on the 24-hour clock?

Ivy knows 12:00 has two different names. Midday is one. What is the other?

....

In a maths lesson, Clara had to write 7.15 a.m. using the 24-hour system. What should she have written?

How many hours are there between 11.30 a.m. and 16:30?

Using the 24-hour clock, write the time one hour before midnight and one hour after midnight.

[ ] and [ ]

Chloe's dad gave her 80 p and her mum gave her double that amount. How much money did Chloe receive in total? Give your answer in pounds and pence.

£2.40

80 x 2 = 160
80 + 160 = 240
100 p = £1.00
so 240 p = £2.40

Noel took 500 1-p coins to the bank and exchanged them for 10-p coins. How many 10-p coins did Noel receive?

coins

After taking £50 out of a cash machine, Olivia had a total of £65.50 on her. How much money did Olivia start with?

Katie wants to buy a jacket and needs to save £20 for it. So far, she has saved £12.50. How much more money does Katie need?

Alex receives £5 pocket money each week. How much money will Alex have after 12 weeks if he doesn't spend any of it?

Liv saved 2-p coins in a bottle. When the bottle was full, she emptied it and counted 270 coins. Calculate Liv's savings. Give your answer in pounds and pence.

Darius wants to buy a CD for £8.99, but he has only £4.60 on him. How much more money does Darius need?

On his way to work, Alison's father filled his car with petrol that cost £38.70. He also paid £3.80 for a newspaper and a coffee. How much did Alison's father spend in total?

```
  38.70
+  3.80
  42.50
```

£42.50

The subscription to an online magazine costs £3.99 a month. How much will a six-month subscription cost?
Note: Look for an easy way to work this out.

✉ Subscribe
Just £3.99 a month!

Adam bought six packets of prawn cocktail flavour crisps for £1.80. How much money did each packet cost? Give your answer in pence.

Riya paid for a train ticket with a £10 note. The ticket cost £7.35. How much change did Riya get back?

☆☆☆ TICKET £7.35

Amit went on a school trip to the zoo. The coach fare was £12.40, the entrance fee was £8.00 and lunch cost £2.70. How much was the cost of the trip?

Annabella bought presents for George on his birthday. They cost her £35. She paid the exact amount with three bank notes. Which three notes did Annabella use?

Length and perimeter problems

The length of a rectangular table top is 60 cm. Its width is 40 cm. What is its perimeter?	Perimeter = (2 x length) + (2 x width)
200 cm	= (2 x 60) + (2 x 40)
	= 120 + 80
	= 200

The distance between London Bridge and the Natural History Museum is 7.4 km. If Peter walks from London Bridge to the museum and back again, how far has he walked?

The perimeter of a rectangle is 30 cm. If the longer side is 8 cm, what is the length of the shorter side?

← 8 cm →

A rectangular car park is 70 m wide and 120 m long. What is the car park's perimeter?

A brick wall, originally 1.88 m high, was lowered in height. If the wall is now 1.49 m high, how much height was lost?

A square has a perimeter of 34 cm. What is the length of each side?

Jack threw a ball a distance of 26.4 m. Then Mary threw the ball and it travelled 29.1 m. How much farther than Jack did Mary throw the ball?

A rectangular bathroom tile is 20 cm long and 8 cm wide. What is its area?

160 cm²

Area = length x width

```
    20
x    8
  ___
   160
```

Sandra needs to buy a sheet of glass measuring 2 m by 3 m to replace a broken window pane. If the glass costs £3.80 per square metre, how much will Sandra need to pay?

A rectangle has an area of 72 cm². If the shorter side of the rectangle is 8 cm, what is the length of the longer side?

A small tin of paint covers 8 m². Kai needs to paint a wall, which is 3 m high and 8 m wide. How many tins of paint will he need?

tins

The length of a rectangle is twice its width. If the area of the rectangle is 32 cm², calculate its length and width.

Length   Width

A rectangular patio is 5 m long and 2 m wide. The materials used to make the patio cost £36 per m² and the workman charged £40 per m² to lay it. How much did the patio cost altogether?

A square has sides of 3 cm. The sides of another square are twice as long. What is the difference in area between the two squares?

★ Fractions

Roger gives one-tenth of his pocket money to charity each week. If he receives £2 pocket money per week, how much of it does he give to charity? Give your answer in pence.

$£1 = 100\,p$

$\frac{1}{10} \times 100 = 10$

so $\frac{1}{10} \times 200 = 20$

20 p

Two-year-old Jemma walked one-fifth of the distance to the shops with her mum. She then became tired and completed the rest of the trip in her buggy. If the total distance was 200 m, how far did Jemma walk and how far did she ride?

Walk [   ]   Ride [   ]

In a packet of sweets, one-eighth are blue and the rest are yellow. What fraction of sweets are yellow?

[   ]

Dev realises that for each hour he works, a quarter of the time is spent daydreaming. If Dev spends two hours working, how much time is not spent daydreaming? Give your answer in hours and minutes.

[   ]

One-third of the children in a class have hot school lunches and the rest have sandwiches. If the class has 27 children, how many have sandwiches for lunch?

[   ] children

Varsha took part in a 400-m race but hurt her ankle after covering just one-fifth of the distance. How far did Varsha run before she was hurt?

[   ]

Zhang paid £10 for lunch and a quarter of that for a soft drink. How much did Zhang pay in total?

[   ]

If 25% of an amount is 15 p, what is the whole amount?	$25\% = \frac{1}{4}$
60 p	$4 \times 15 = 60$

Rob spends 50% of his time at the gym swimming and the rest on cardio exercises. If Rob spends three hours at the gym, how much time does he spend on each activity? Give your answer in hours and minutes.

The chances of winning with a lottery ticket are 1 in 10. What is that as a fraction and a percentage?

On a day trip to Edinburgh, Mrs and Mr Harris spent 25% of their money on each of their three children. They spent the rest of the money on themselves. If £25 was spent on each child, how much did Mrs and Mr Harris spend in total?

A car covered a total of 180 miles. After the first 20 miles, the car had a flat tyre. What fraction of the journey had already taken place when the puncture happened?

Russell calculated that one-eighth of the footballers in the Football League are French. If the League has 240 players, how many of them are not French?

players

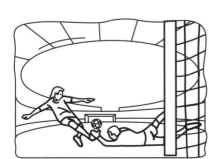

On her seventh birthday, Morgan was 1.25 m tall.
By her eighth birthday, she had grown by 0.16 m.
How tall was Morgan on her eighth birthday?

$$\begin{array}{r} 1.25 \\ +\ \ 0.16 \\ \hline 1.41 \end{array}$$

1.41 m

Between the ages of 2 and 18, Matthew doubled in height. If Matthew was 0.88 m tall at the age of 2, how tall was he at the age of 18?

Every day, Madeleine's horse eats 2.5 kg of oats. How many kilograms of oats does the horse eat in one week?

Change each fraction to its decimal equivalent.

$\frac{3}{4}$  $\frac{1}{2}$  $\frac{1}{4}$

A cola bottle holds 1 l of the drink. If Danni and her friends drank 0.75 l, how much was left?

Stephen wants to get in shape for an upcoming sports tournament.
He weighs 50 kg now and wants to reduce his weight by 2.5 kg.
If Stephen is successful, what will be his new weight?

A packet of peanuts that usually costs £2 was reduced by 0.25. What is the new price of the packet?

£1.50

$0.25 = \frac{1}{4}$

$\frac{1}{4} \times 2 = 0.50$

$$\begin{array}{r} 2.00 \\ - \ 0.50 \\ \hline 1.50 \end{array}$$

A bag contained 12 apples. The next day, 0.25 of the apples were eaten. How many apples were left?

apples

Tabitha bought a box of chocolates, of which 0.75 were milk and the rest were plain. If the box had 24 chocolates, how many were plain and how many were milk chocolates?

plain chocolates   milk chocolates

Change each fraction to its decimal equivalent.

$\frac{1}{5}$ $\frac{1}{10}$ $\frac{7}{10}$

Alexander's garden path was doubled in length to 7.8 m. What was the length of the original path?

If 0.75 of a number is 12, what is the number?

Clara usually receives £4 pocket money each week. This week, however, her father gave her an extra 0.2 of that amount for helping with the preparations for a weekend party. How much extra money did Clara receive? Give your answer in pence.

On Harry's birthday, Gina gave him a card that said, 'Happy Birthday! You're now XVIII'. How old is Harry?

 18 | years

X = 10
V = 5
I = 1
10 + 5 + 3 = 18

An old-fashioned clock shows the hour hand pointing at VI and the minute hand at XII. What is the time?

These shields show the numbers of three Roman legions. How would we write these numbers?

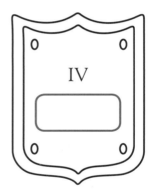

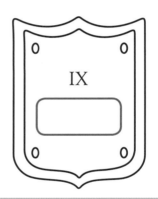

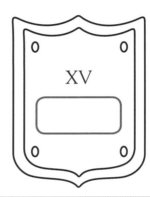

Using Roman numerals, write the number that is one less than each of these.

III   X   XX

Work out these sums using Roman numerals. Write the answers in numbers.

L + X + V + I =   VI + IX + L =

LXII – XX =   LXV – XIII =

Write each of these numbers in its Roman form.

15   56   24

In a running club, the ratio of boys to girls is 2:1. If the club has 40 boys, how many girls are there in the club?

| 20 | girls

2:1 means there are twice as many boys as girls, so

40 ÷ 2 = 20

The ratio of girls to boys in a school show was 2:1. If there were 20 girls in the show, how many children were involved altogether?

| | children

For a school project, Kai asked 24 sports fans to name their favourite sport. The result was 3:1 in favour of football over rugby. How many fans preferred each sport?

Football | | Rugby | |

In a class of 30 children, 20 have brown hair and the rest have blond hair. What is the ratio of brown to blond-haired children in the class?
Note: Write the ratio as simply as possible.

| |

A box of assorted sweets contains the flavours grape, watermelon and strawberry in the ratio of 3:2:1. If there are 9 grape-flavoured sweets, how many watermelon and strawberry-flavoured sweets are there in the box?

| | watermelon flavour | | strawberry flavour

In a car showroom, there are silver cars and red cars in the ratio of 1:4. If there are 16 red cars, how many cars does the showroom have in total?

| | cars

The ratio of cows to sheep on Tom's farm is 2:3. If the farm has a total of 40 cows and sheep, how many are there of each type of animal?

| | cows | | sheep

This chart shows how many times boys and girls borrowed books from a school library. Look carefully and answer the questions.

Title (Author)	Boys	Girls
Max's Secret Diary (Joan Kennedy)	640	295
My Grandmother's Story (Heath Murphy)	566	531
Amazon to London: Sam's Adventure (Suzie Ray)	170	462
The Dragon and the Unicorn (David Wahlberg)	602	583

Which author was the most popular with boys?

....

Which author was the most popular with girls?

....

Which book was borrowed the most?

....

Which book had the biggest difference between the number of boy readers and the number of girl readers?

....

How many more times was *My Grandmother's Story* borrowed than *Max's Secret Diary*?

[   ] times

Which author had a book borrowed 632 times?

....

A class of schoolchildren in Canterbury voted for their favourite television channel. Look at the pie chart and then answer the questions.

Most popular television channels

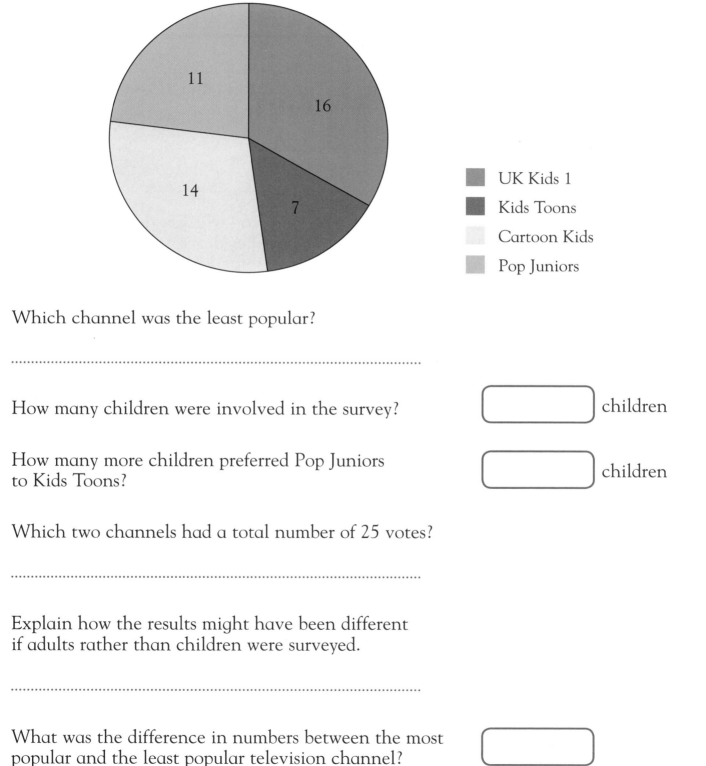

UK Kids 1
Kids Toons
Cartoon Kids
Pop Juniors

Which channel was the least popular?

....

How many children were involved in the survey? [   ] children

How many more children preferred Pop Juniors to Kids Toons? [   ] children

Which two channels had a total number of 25 votes?

....

Explain how the results might have been different if adults rather than children were surveyed.

....

What was the difference in numbers between the most popular and the least popular television channel? [   ]

The sum of two numbers is 75. One number is 18. What is the other number? **Note:** This problem can be solved in different ways.	75 – 18 = 57 or 18 + **2** = 20 20 + **50** = 70 70 + **5** = 75 **2** + **50** + **5** = 57
57	

Last month, Sebastian delivered parcels to four shops in Bond Street. He delivered 12 parcels to one shop, 37 to the next shop, 28 to the third and 31 to the final shop. How many parcels did Sebastian deliver altogether?

☐ parcels

For their last holiday, the Robinsons went on a long road trip. On the first day of their holiday, they drove 190 km. On the second day they drove 165 km and on the final day they drove 85 km. How many kilometres in total did the Robinsons travel?

☐

Amal put her building blocks into three piles according to their colours, which were red, blue and yellow. There were 20 blocks in the red pile and 35 blocks in the blue pile. If Amal has a total of 100 blocks, how many yellow blocks did she have?

☐ yellow blocks

Xavier challenged Liam to a computer game. Liam scored 200 points. However, Xavier beat Liam's score by 130 points. How many points did Xavier score?

☐ points

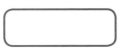

The difference between two numbers is 17.
The larger number is 50. What is the smaller number?

☐

Forty-nine people auditioned for a dance company over two days. If 26 people were selected on the first day and four more on the second day, how many people were not chosen?

$$26 + 4 = 30$$

$$\begin{array}{r} 49 \\ -30 \\ \hline 19 \end{array}$$

19 people

When three numbers are added together, the total is 150.
Two of the numbers are 20 and 35. What is the third number?

When two different numbers are added together, their total is 12.
If one of the numbers is double the other, what are the two numbers?

and

The United Nations, or UN, has 193 member countries. Of these, 51 countries were original members of the organisation. How many member countries are not original members of the UN?

countries

Four classes from Knightwood Primary School went on a school picnic.
The number of children and helpers for each class were 37, 36, 29 and 38.
What was the total number of children and helpers at the picnic?

children and helpers

For a science fair, Beatrice made a working model of a drawbridge.
The model was made up of 73 different pieces, of which 34 pieces were metal and the rest plastic. How many plastic pieces did Beatrice use in her model?

plastic pieces

Daniel played a new game on his computer. He had three tries and achieved the same score each time. If Daniel had scored a total of 27 points, how many points did he score in each try?

$27 \div 3 = 9$

[9] points

Guests at Rupert's party were seated at tables of eight. If 56 guests attended the party, how many tables did Rupert need for his guests?

[ ] tables

The fence panels Harriet bought for her garden are sold in packs of four. If Harriet used 36 panels, how many packs did she buy?

[ ] packs

A decade is the same as 10 years. How many decades are the same as 110 years?

[ ] decades

A number is multiplied by itself and the answer is then doubled. If the final number is 50, what was the original number?

[ ]

Schoolchildren at Gilmore Academy took part in a cross-country race. They were divided into groups of nine. If there were seven groups in the race, how many children took part?

[ ] children

Lillian made a large cube out of small cubes. Each edge of the large cube was four times the length of the edge of a small cube. How many small cubes were used to make the large cube?

[ ] small cubes

Johanna bought a pack of 24 crayons and shared them out equally among her six nieces and nephews. How many crayons did each child receive?

$24 \div 6 = 4$

| 4 | crayons

In a school week, Peter does eight sums for homework each night. If the school week lasts five days, how many sums does Peter have to do each week?

| | sums

Last year, Daisy's summer holiday lasted a total of five weeks and three days. Calculate Daisy's holiday in days.

| | days

Johnny thought of a number and then doubled it. He then doubled the new number and arrived at a final answer of 32. What was Johnny's original number?

| |

A mystery number when divided by 12 gives nine as the result. What is the mystery number?

| |

Marianne bought a box of cereal that contained 24 wheat biscuits. If she ate two wheat biscuits every day, how many days did the biscuits last?

| | days

Each window display in a large clothes shop in London has three mannequins. If the shop has nine window displays, how many mannequins are there in total?

| | mannequins

The perimeter of a rectangle is 26 cm and its width is 4 cm. Calculate its length.	Perimeter = (2 x length) + (2 x width) 2 x 4 taken away from 26 will give you twice the length.
9 cm	26 – 8 = 18 18 ÷ 2 = 9

At a shopping centre, Ava paid the £1.65 fee for parking with coins.
She used the fewest number of coins to give the exact amount.
What were they?

The perimeter of a rectangle is 18 cm. The shorter side of the rectangle is half the length of the longer side. What are the lengths of the sides?

[   ] and [   ]

A bowl contains 36 pieces of fruit. One-sixth of them are oranges.
How many pieces of fruit in the bowl are not oranges?

[   ] pieces of fruit

Out of 90 contestants in a talent show, 10% danced and the rest sang.
How many contestants sang?

[   ]

The distance between Wigan and Birch Green is 8.9 miles. What is the total distance travelled if you go from Wigan to Birch Green and then back again?

[   ]

In his wardrobe, Julian has ties and shirts in the ratio of 1:5. If Julian has a total of 18 ties and shirts, how many does he have of each?

[   ] ties   [   ] shirts

A standard running track is 400 m. If a runner runs around the track four times, how much distance has she covered? **Note:** Write the answer in kilometres.	400 x 4 1600
1.6 km	1 km = 1000 m so 1600 m = 1.6 km

The year CLV, written in Roman numerals, was a very long time ago. When was it?

Richard won the lottery but gave 75% of it away to charity. If Richard won £100 000, how much did he give to charity?

A grocer needs to stock 96 apples in his store. If apples come in bags of 12, how many bags does he need?

bags

A rectangle has sides of 7 cm and 4 cm and a square has sides of 5 cm. Which shape has the larger area and by how much?

A bus arrives at a stop every 25 minutes. If the first bus arrives at 11:45, at what time will the next three buses arrive? Give your answers using the 24-hour system.

In a fruit bowl, the ratio of oranges to bananas is 3:1. If the bowl has four bananas, how many oranges are there?

oranges

Cleo went to a shop to buy new trainers. She liked a pair that cost £87. However, she used a discount voucher and only had to pay £42.70. How much did Cleo save?

```
  87.00
– 42.70
  44.30
```

£44.30

Trinny follows the same exercise regime every day. She jogs 1.3 km at a steady pace every 15 minutes. What time does Trinny finish if she leaves home at 15:40 every day and jogs a total distance of 6.5 km? Give your answer using the 24-hour system.

What is the area of the shape on the right?

5 cm
5 cm
2 cm
12 cm

The cost of posting a parcel depends on its weight. If a parcel weighing 2 kg costs £2.80 to post, what will a parcel weighing 10 kg cost?

Mila tiled her bathroom floor. For each green tile she used, she used five white tiles. If Mila used 30 tiles, how many of each colour did she use?

Green ☐   White ☐

The perimeter of a regular hexagon is 78 cm. What is the length of each side?

Sean multiplied a number by itself and then halved it. The result was 24.5. Which number did Sean start with?

A number is 0.6 higher than another number. If the larger number is 6.1, what is the smaller number?

> 6.1
> − 0.6
> 5.5

5.5

Two numbers are added together to make 7.4. If one of the numbers is 4.9, what is the other number?

One number is twice as big as another number. If the total of the two numbers is 9.3, what are the two numbers?

and

A number is doubled and then three is added to it. If the final number is 5.8, what was the original number?

A rectangular lawn is 3.8 m long and 2.6 m wide. What is the perimeter of the lawn?

Jonathan is 1.84 m tall and his sister Lana is 1.46 m tall. Their older sister Katya's height is exactly halfway between the two heights. Calculate Katya's height.

If the centre of a circle is 4.6 cm from the edge of the circle, what is the distance all the way across the circle?

What is three-fifths of 30?	$\frac{1}{5}$ of 30 = 30 ÷ 5 = 6
18	so $\frac{3}{5}$ will be 3 x 6 = 18

Spencer bought a bag of mixed lily bulbs to plant in his garden. The bag contained 24 bulbs. When they flowered, three-eighths of the lilies were red and the rest were yellow. How many lilies were yellow?

☐ lilies

In a survey of 60 drivers, three-tenths said they had passed their driving test the first time. How many drivers in the survey did not pass the first time?

☐ drivers

Parker and his friends hiked 180 m up a hill. They stopped to rest after completing two-thirds of the way. How much farther did they hike after their rest?

☐

A doctor spends five-sixths of each hour seeing patients and the rest of the hour writing notes. How many minutes does she spend writing notes each hour?

☐

How long is three-quarters of two hours in minutes?

☐

Donovan was given £1 for helping his dad in the garden. He saved two-fifths of the amount. How much money did he save? Give your answer in pence.

☐

Answer section with parents' notes

Key Stage 2
Ages 7–9

This eight-page section provides answers and explanatory notes to all the problems in this book, enabling you to assess your child's work.

Work through each page together and ensure that your child understands each maths problem. Point out any mistakes your child makes and correct the errors. Your child should use the methods of working out taught at his or her school. In addition to making corrections, it is very important to praise your child's efforts and achievements.

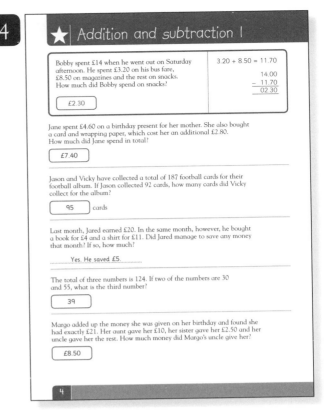

★ Addition and subtraction 1

Bobby spent £14 when he went out on Saturday afternoon. He spent £3.20 on his bus fare, £8.50 on magazines and the rest on snacks. How much did Bobby spend on snacks?

$3.20 + 8.50 = 11.70$

$$\begin{array}{r} 14.00 \\ - 11.70 \\ \hline 02.30 \end{array}$$

£2.30

Jane spent £4.60 on a birthday present for her mother. She also bought a card and wrapping paper, which cost her an additional £2.80. How much did Jane spend in total?

£7.40

Jason and Vicky have collected a total of 187 football cards for their football album. If Jason collected 92 cards, how many cards did Vicky collect for the album?

95 cards

Last month, Jared earned £20. In the same month, however, he bought a book for £4 and a shirt for £11. Did Jared manage to save any money that month? If so, how much?

Yes. He saved £5.

The total of three numbers is 124. If two of the numbers are 30 and 55, what is the third number?

39

Margo added up the money she was given on her birthday and found she had exactly £21. Her aunt gave her £10, her sister gave her £2.50 and her uncle gave her the rest. How much money did Margo's uncle give her?

£8.50

Including units in each step of the working out of a problem is useful when you need to convert from one unit to another, such as pounds to pence. Even if you don't use units in working out, always include them in your final answers.

Addition and subtraction 2 ★

Ian organised an anniversary party for his parents. He sent out 84 invites, but only 67 people confirmed. On the day of the party, however, 7 more of those who were invited turned up. How many invited people did not attend the party?

$67 + 7 = 74$

$$\begin{array}{r} 84 \\ - 74 \\ \hline 10 \end{array}$$

10 people

In a class of 31 children, 8 have blue eyes, 19 have brown eyes and the rest have green eyes. How many children in the class have green eyes?

4 children

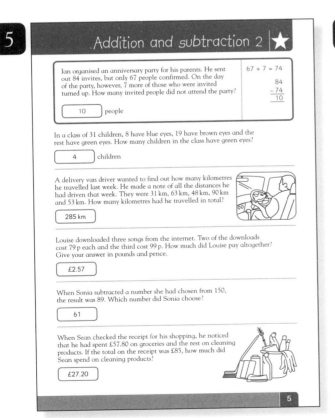

A delivery van driver wanted to find out how many kilometres he travelled last week. He made a note of all the distances he had driven that week. They were 31 km, 63 km, 48 km, 90 km and 53 km. How many kilometres had he travelled in total?

285 km

Louise downloaded three songs from the internet. Two of the downloads cost 79 p each and the third cost 99 p. How much did Louise pay altogether? Give your answer in pounds and pence.

£2.57

When Sonia subtracted a number she had chosen from 150, the result was 89. Which number did Sonia choose?

61

When Sean checked the receipt for his shopping, he noticed that he had spent £57.80 on groceries and the rest on cleaning products. If the total on the receipt was £85, how much did Sean spend on cleaning products?

£27.20

Your child may have been taught different methods of addition and subtraction, as schools have their own teaching methods. To provide the best guidance, find out these methods by talking to your child or her/his teacher.

★ Times tables 1

What is two times two times two?

8

$2 \times 2 = 4$
$4 \times 2 = 8$

If four eights are 32, what will eight eights be?

64

How many days are the same as eight weeks?

56 days

If 12 fours are 48, what will six fours be?

24

Double four and then double it again. What is the answer?

16

Emily halves a number and the result is 16. What was the original number that she chose?

32

When five is multiplied by a mystery number, the answer is 60. What is the mystery number?

12

If 12 times 12 is 144, what will six times 12 be?

72

Encourage your child to learn times tables by helping him/her realise that when he/she is learning one times table, he/she is actually learning two! Explain that if 3 x 5 is 15, he/she also knows that 5 x 3 is 15.

Times tables 2 ⭐

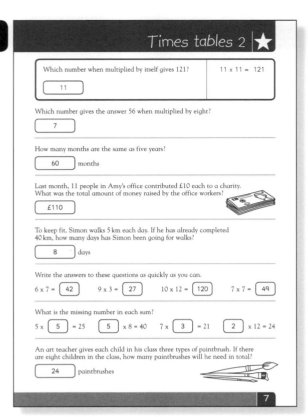

Which number when multiplied by itself gives 121?	11 x 11 = 121
11	

Which number gives the answer 56 when multiplied by eight?

7

How many months are the same as five years?

60 months

Last month, 11 people in Amy's office contributed £10 each to a charity. What was the total amount of money raised by the office workers?

£110

To keep fit, Simon walks 5 km each day. If he has already completed 40 km, how many days has Simon been going for walks?

8 days

Write the answers to these questions as quickly as you can.

6 x 7 = 42   9 x 3 = 27   10 x 12 = 120   7 x 7 = 49

What is the missing number in each sum?

5 x 5 = 25   5 x 8 = 40   7 x 3 = 21   2 x 12 = 24

An art teacher gives each child in his class three types of paintbrush. If there are eight children in the class, how many paintbrushes will he need in total?

24 paintbrushes

7

Ask your child to choose a times table and recite it to you. Not only will it be a good practice for her/him but it will also show you how well she/he is progressing.

⭐ Multiplication and division 1

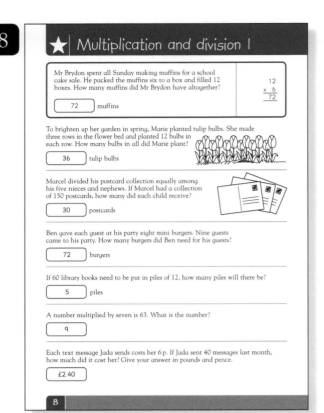

Mr Brydon spent all Sunday making muffins for a school cake sale. He packed the muffins six to a box and filled 12 boxes. How many muffins did Mr Brydon have altogether?	12 x 6 72
72 muffins	

To brighten up her garden in spring, Marie planted tulip bulbs. She made three rows in the flower bed and planted 12 bulbs in each row. How many bulbs in all did Marie plant?

36 tulip bulbs

Marcel divided his postcard collection equally among his five nieces and nephews. If Marcel had a collection of 150 postcards, how many did each child receive?

30 postcards

Ben gave each guest at his party eight mini burgers. Nine guests came to his party. How many burgers did Ben need for his guests?

72 burgers

If 60 library books need to be put in piles of 12, how many piles will there be?

5 piles

A number multiplied by seven is 63. What is the number?

9

Each text message Jada sends costs her 6 p. If Jada sent 40 messages last month, how much did it cost her? Give your answer in pounds and pence.

£2.40

8

The concepts of multiplication and division are closely related. They are, in fact, the "inverse" of each other. Tell your child if 3 x 4 = 12, then 12 ÷ 3 = 4 and 12 ÷ 4 = 3. Understanding this will make working with them easier.

Multiplication and division 2 ⭐

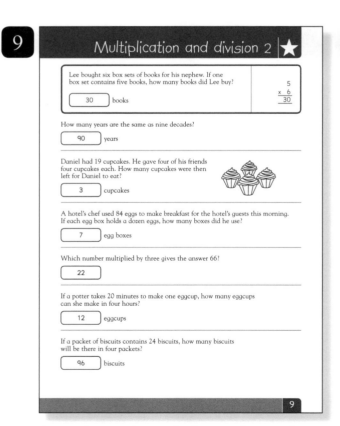

Lee bought six box sets of books for his nephew. If one box set contains five books, how many books did Lee buy?	5 x 6 30
30 books	

How many years are the same as nine decades?

90 years

Daniel had 19 cupcakes. He gave four of his friends four cupcakes each. How many cupcakes were then left for Daniel to eat?

3 cupcakes

A hotel's chef used 84 eggs to make breakfast for the hotel's guests this morning. If each egg box holds a dozen eggs, how many boxes did he use?

7 egg boxes

Which number multiplied by three gives the answer 66?

22

If a potter takes 20 minutes to make one eggcup, how many eggcups can she make in four hours?

12 eggcups

If a packet of biscuits contains 24 biscuits, how many biscuits will be there in four packets?

96 biscuits

9

As numbers used in multiplication become larger, such as 16 x 8 rather than 3 x 4, the methods for working out the problem also change. If your child is unsure how to work with larger numbers, ask her teacher about the methods taught.

⭐ Time problems 1

For breakfast, Dan likes to boil his eggs for four-and-a-half minutes. How long is that in seconds?	1 minute = 60 seconds 4 x 60 = 240 ½ minute = 30 seconds
270 seconds	240 + 30 270

Emma went shopping at 10.00 a.m. and returned at 2.30 p.m. How long did Emma shop for? Give your answer in hours and minutes.

4 hours 30 minutes

Harris likes to tell his age in months instead of years. If Harris is six-and-a-half years old, how would he say his age?

78 months

George has been alive for five-and-a-half decades. How old is George in years?

55 years

Which two months in a row have 31 days?

July and August or January and December

While swimming, David managed to do the front crawl for 11 seconds, while Taylor managed to do it for 20 seconds. How much longer than David did Taylor manage to do the crawl?

9 seconds

It took Elizabeth 35 minutes to walk to Winchester's city centre from her home. If Elizabeth left her home at 8.45 a.m., what time did she reach the city centre?

9.20 a.m.

10

Help your child understand how the units of time relate to each other. Start with the number of seconds in a minute, moving on to the number of minutes in an hour, hours in a day and the number of days in the different months.

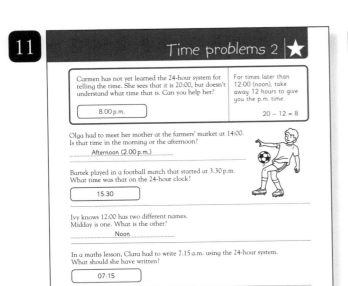

11 — Time problems 2 ★

Carmen has not yet learned the 24-hour system for telling the time. She sees that it is 20:00, but doesn't understand what time that is. Can you help her?

8.00 p.m.

For times later than 12:00 (noon), take away 12 hours to give you the p.m. time.

20 − 12 = 8

Olga had to meet her mother at the farmers' market at 14:00. Is that time in the morning or the afternoon?

Afternoon (2.00 p.m.)

Bartek played in a football match that started at 3.30 p.m. What time was that on the 24-hour clock?

15:30

Ivy knows 12:00 has two different names. Midday is one. What is the other?

Noon

In a maths lesson, Clara had to write 7.15 a.m. using the 24-hour system. What should she have written?

07:15

How many hours are there between 11.30 a.m. and 16:30?

5 hours

Using the 24-hour clock, write the time one hour before midnight and one hour after midnight.

23:00 and **01:00**

Children usually learn the 24-hour system by looking at devices, such as mobiles and tablets. Where possible, change the display of the clock from 12 hour to 24 hour, to make sure your child knows how the two systems are related.

12 — ★ Money problems 1

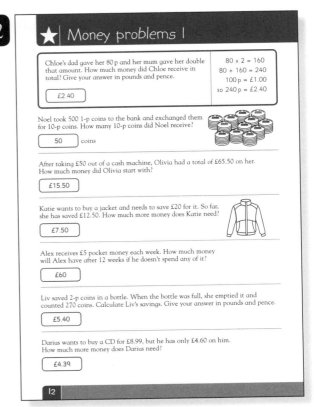

Chloe's dad gave her 80 p and her mum gave her double that amount. How much money did Chloe receive in total? Give your answer in pounds and pence.

£2.40

80 × 2 = 160
80 + 160 = 240
100 p = £1.00
so 240 p = £2.40

Noel took 500 1-p coins to the bank and exchanged them for 10-p coins. How many 10-p coins did Noel receive?

50 coins

After taking £50 out of a cash machine, Olivia had a total of £65.50 on her. How much money did Olivia start with?

£15.50

Katie wants to buy a jacket and needs to save £20 for it. So far, she has saved £12.50. How much more money does Katie need?

£7.50

Alex receives £5 pocket money each week. How much money will Alex have after 12 weeks if he doesn't spend any of it?

£60

Liv saved 2-p coins in a bottle. When the bottle was full, she emptied it and counted 270 coins. Calculate Liv's savings. Give your answer in pounds and pence.

£5.40

Darius wants to buy a CD for £8.99, but he has only £4.60 on him. How much more money does Darius need?

£4.39

Your child will understand money better if you give him the opportunity to see and handle money in real situations.

13 — Money problems 2 ★

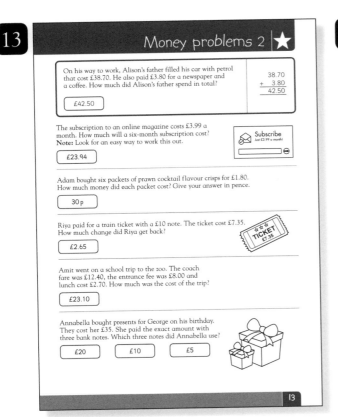

On his way to work, Alison's father filled his car with petrol that cost £38.70. He also paid £3.80 for a newspaper and a coffee. How much did Alison's father spend in total?

£42.50

```
  38.70
+  3.80
 ------
  42.50
```

The subscription to an online magazine costs £3.99 a month. How much will a six-month subscription cost?
Note: Look for an easy way to work this out.

£23.94

Adam bought six packets of prawn cocktail flavour crisps for £1.80. How much money did each packet cost? Give your answer in pence.

30 p

Riya paid for a train ticket with a £10 note. The ticket cost £7.35. How much change did Riya get back?

£2.65

Amit went on a school trip to the zoo. The coach fare was £12.40, the entrance fee was £8.00 and lunch cost £2.70. How much was the cost of the trip?

£23.10

Annabella bought presents for George on his birthday. They cost her £35. She paid the exact amount with three bank notes. Which three notes did Annabella use?

£20   **£10**   **£5**

Ensure your child is familiar with all the coins and notes in the UK currency. Also, introduce her to the euro and the US dollar. Discuss how the main units are divided and how these compare with UK currency.

14 — ★ Length and perimeter problems

The length of a rectangular table top is 60 cm. Its width is 40 cm. What is its perimeter?

200 cm

Perimeter = (2 × length) + (2 × width)
= (2 × 60) + (2 × 40)
= 120 + 80
= 200

The distance between London Bridge and the Natural History Museum is 7.4 km. If Peter walks from London Bridge to the museum and back again, how far has he walked?

14.8 km

The perimeter of a rectangle is 30 cm. If the longer side is 8 cm, what is the length of the shorter side?

7 cm

A rectangular car park is 70 m wide and 120 m long. What is the car park's perimeter?

380 m

A brick wall, originally 1.88 m high, was lowered in height. If the wall is now 1.49 m high, how much height was lost?

0.39 m

A square has a perimeter of 34 cm. What is the length of each side?

8.5 cm

Jack threw a ball a distance of 26.4 m. Then Mary threw the ball and it travelled 29.1 m. How much farther than Jack did Mary throw the ball?

2.7 m

Your child should be able to describe metric units of length, such as the millimetre and centimetre, by using his hands. For example, a millimetre is about the length of the free edge of a fingernail and a centimetre is about the width of a finger.

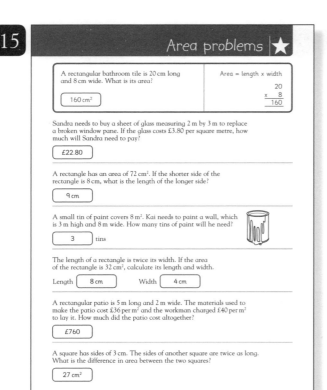

A rectangular bathroom tile is 20 cm long and 8 cm wide. What is its area?

160 cm²

Area = length x width

20
x   8
160

Sandra needs to buy a sheet of glass measuring 2 m by 3 m to replace a broken window pane. If the glass costs £3.80 per square metre, how much will Sandra need to pay?

£22.80

A rectangle has an area of 72 cm². If the shorter side of the rectangle is 8 cm, what is the length of the longer side?

9 cm

A small tin of paint covers 8 m². Kai needs to paint a wall, which is 3 m high and 8 m wide. How many tins of paint will he need?

3   tins

The length of a rectangle is twice its width. If the area of the rectangle is 32 cm², calculate its length and width.

Length   8 cm   Width   4 cm

A rectangular patio is 5 m long and 2 m wide. The materials used to make the patio cost £36 per m² and the workman charged £40 per m² to lay it. How much did the patio cost altogether?

£760

A square has sides of 3 cm. The sides of another square are twice as long. What is the difference in area between the two squares?

27 cm²

15

Make sure that your child understands the more general concept of area – that it is the amount of space inside a flat shape. For practice, ask her/him to find the areas of simple squares and rectangles.

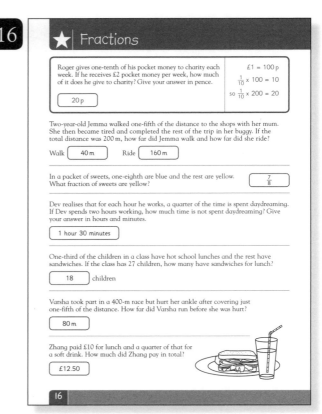

Roger gives one-tenth of his pocket money to charity each week. If he receives £2 pocket money per week, how much of it does he give to charity? Give your answer in pence.

20 p

£1 = 100 p

$\frac{1}{10}$ x 100 = 10

so $\frac{1}{10}$ x 200 = 20

Two-year-old Jemma walked one-fifth of the distance to the shops with her mum. She then became tired and completed the rest of the trip in her buggy. If the total distance was 200 m, how far did Jemma walk and how far did she ride?

Walk   40 m   Ride   160 m

In a packet of sweets, one-eighth are blue and the rest are yellow. What fraction of sweets are yellow?

$\frac{7}{8}$

Dev realises that for each hour he works, a quarter of the time is spent daydreaming. If Dev spends two hours working, how much time is not spent daydreaming? Give your answer in hours and minutes.

1 hour 30 minutes

One-third of the children in a class have hot school lunches and the rest have sandwiches. If the class has 27 children, how many have sandwiches for lunch?

18   children

Varsha took part in a 400-m race but hurt her ankle after covering just one-fifth of the distance. How far did Varsha run before she was hurt?

80 m

Zhang paid £10 for lunch and a quarter of that for a soft drink. How much did Zhang pay in total?

£12.50

16

It is important for your child to understand the connection between unitary fractions and times tables. For example, if one-third of 24 is required, then the three times tables is involved.

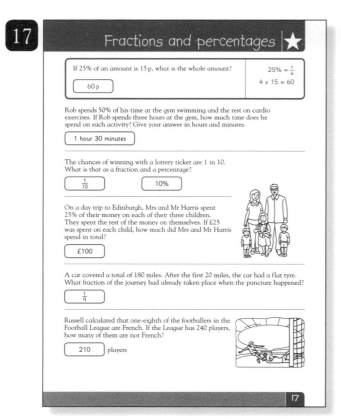

If 25% of an amount is 15 p, what is the whole amount?

60 p

25% = $\frac{1}{4}$

4 x 15 = 60

Rob spends 50% of his time at the gym swimming and the rest on cardio exercises. If Rob spends three hours at the gym, how much time does he spend on each activity? Give your answer in hours and minutes.

1 hour 30 minutes

The chances of winning with a lottery ticket are 1 in 10. What is that as a fraction and a percentage?

$\frac{1}{10}$ 10%

On a day trip to Edinburgh, Mrs and Mr Harris spent 25% of their money on each of their three children. They spent the rest of the money on themselves. If £25 was spent on each child, how much did Mrs and Mr Harris spend in total?

£100

A car covered a total of 180 miles. After the first 20 miles, the car had a flat tyre. What fraction of the journey had already taken place when the puncture happened?

$\frac{1}{9}$

Russell calculated that one-eighth of the footballers in the Football League are French. If the League has 240 players, how many of them are not French?

210   players

17

Conversion between simple fractions and their percentage equivalents is important to learn. For example, $\frac{1}{2}$ is the same as 50%, $\frac{1}{5}$ is 20% and so on. Your child should also learn the more complex ones, such as $\frac{1}{3}$ equalling 33.3%.

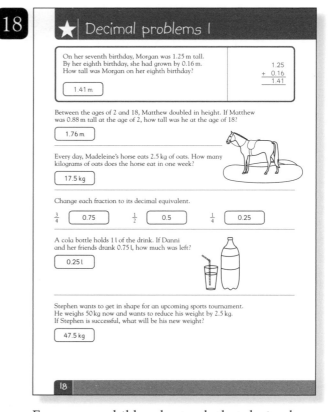

On her seventh birthday, Morgan was 1.25 m tall. By her eighth birthday, she had grown by 0.16 m. How tall was Morgan on her eighth birthday?

1.41 m

1.25
+ 0.16
1.41

Between the ages of 2 and 18, Matthew doubled in height. If Matthew was 0.88 m tall at the age of 2, how tall was he at the age of 18?

1.76 m

Every day, Madeleine's horse eats 2.5 kg of oats. How many kilograms of oats does the horse eat in one week?

17.5 kg

Change each fraction to its decimal equivalent.

$\frac{3}{4}$ 0.75 $\frac{1}{2}$ 0.5 $\frac{1}{4}$ 0.25

A cola bottle holds 1 l of the drink. If Danni and her friends drank 0.75 l, how much was left?

0.25 l

Stephen wants to get in shape for an upcoming sports tournament. He weighs 50 kg now and wants to reduce his weight by 2.5 kg. If Stephen is successful, what will be his new weight?

47.5 kg

18

Ensure your child understands that decimals can be another way of showing numbers less than one. To begin with, teach him that 0.5 is a half and then explain that an amount less than 0.5 will be less than half and so on.

Decimal problems 2 ★

A packet of peanuts that usually costs £2 was reduced by 0.25. What is the new price of the packet?

$0.25 = \frac{1}{4}$
$\frac{1}{4} \times 2 = 0.50$

| £1.50 |

$$\begin{array}{r} 2.00 \\ -\ 0.50 \\ \hline 1.50 \end{array}$$

A bag contained 12 apples. The next day, 0.25 of the apples were eaten. How many apples were left?

| 9 | apples

Tabitha bought a box of chocolates, of which 0.75 were milk and the rest were plain. If the box had 24 chocolates, how many were plain and how many were milk chocolates?

| 6 | plain chocolates | 18 | milk chocolates

Change each fraction to its decimal equivalent.

$\frac{1}{5}$ | 0.2 | $\frac{1}{10}$ | 0.1 | $\frac{7}{10}$ | 0.7 |

Alexander's garden path was doubled in length to 7.8 m. What was the length of the original path?

| 3.9 m |

If 0.75 of a number is 12, what is the number?

| 16 |

Clara usually receives £4 pocket money each week. This week, however, her father gave her an extra 0.2 of that amount for helping with the preparations for a weekend party. How much extra money did Clara receive? Give your answer in pence.

| 80 p |

Some of the problems on this page involve numbers with two decimal places. Your child will encounter such decimals in day-to-day life when using money (for example, £2.99) or measuring lengths (for example, 1.43 m).

★ Roman numerals

On Harry's birthday, Gina gave him a card that said, 'Happy Birthday! You're now XVIII'. How old is Harry?

| 18 | years

X = 10
V = 5
I = 1
10 + 5 + 3 = 18

An old-fashioned clock shows the hour hand pointing at VI and the minute hand at XII. What is the time?

| 6 o'clock |

These shields show the numbers of three Roman legions. How would we write these numbers?

IV | 4 | IX | 9 | XV | 15 |

Using Roman numerals, write the number that is one less than each of these.

III | II | X | IX | XX | XIX |

Work out these sums using Roman numerals. Write the answers in numbers.

L + X + V + I = | 66 | VI + IX + L = | 65 |

LXII – XX = | 42 | LXV – XIII = | 52 |

Write each of these numbers in its Roman form.

15 | XV | 56 | LVI | 24 | XXIV |

Children usually find Roman numerals interesting, so look out for real-life examples, such as on clocks, in music notation and in the closing credits of some television programmes and films.

Ratio problems ★

In a running club, the ratio of boys to girls is 2:1. If the club has 40 boys, how many girls are there in the club?

| 20 | girls

2:1 means there are twice as many boys as girls, so 40 ÷ 2 = 20

The ratio of girls to boys in a school show was 2:1. If there were 20 girls in the show, how many children were involved altogether?

| 30 | children

For a school project, Kai asked 24 sports fans to name their favourite sport. The result was 3:1 in favour of football over rugby. How many fans preferred each sport?

Football | 18 | Rugby | 6 |

In a class of 30 children, 20 have brown hair and the rest have blond hair. What is the ratio of brown to blond-haired children in the class?
Note: Write the ratio as simply as possible.

| 2:1 |

A box of assorted sweets contains the flavours grape, watermelon and strawberry in the ratio of 3:2:1. If there are 9 grape-flavoured sweets, how many watermelon and strawberry-flavoured sweets are there in the box?

| 6 | watermelon flavour | 3 | strawberry flavour

In a car showroom, there are silver cars and red cars in the ratio of 1:4. If there are 16 red cars, how many cars does the showroom have in total?

| 20 | cars

The ratio of cows to sheep on Tom's farm is 2:3. If the farm has a total of 40 cows and sheep, how many are there of each type of animal?

| 16 | cows | 24 | sheep

Encourage your child to think of ratios as a way of showing the proportions between amounts in a group. For example, 2:3 may be thought of as "for every two parts, there are three other parts".

★ Understanding charts 1

This chart shows how many times boys and girls borrowed books from a school library. Look carefully and answer the questions.

Title (Author)	Boys	Girls
Max's Secret Diary (Joan Kennedy)	640	295
My Grandmother's Story (Heath Murphy)	566	531
Amazon to London: Sam's Adventure (Suzie Ray)	170	462
The Dragon and the Unicorn (David Wahlberg)	602	583

Which author was the most popular with boys?
Joan Kennedy

Which author was the most popular with girls?
David Wahlberg

Which book was borrowed the most?
The Dragon and the Unicorn

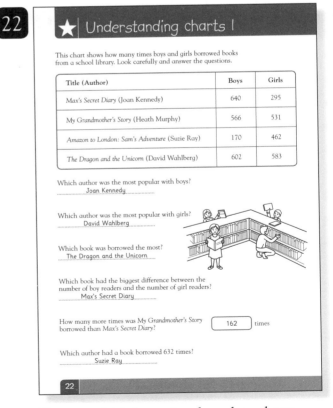

Which book had the biggest difference between the number of boy readers and the number of girl readers?
Max's Secret Diary

How many more times was My Grandmother's Story borrowed than Max's Secret Diary? | 162 | times

Which author had a book borrowed 632 times?
Suzie Ray

To get useful information from data charts, your child should study them very carefully. When tackling the questions, he/she should not make any assumptions about what is being asked and read each one twice.

23 — Understanding charts 2 ★

A class of schoolchildren in Canterbury voted for their favourite television channel. Look at the pie chart and then answer the questions.

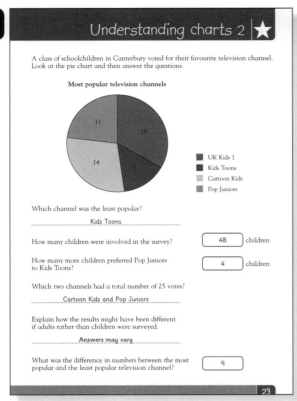

Most popular television channels

- ■ UK Kids 1
- ■ Kids Toons
- ▨ Cartoon Kids
- ▨ Pop Juniors

Which channel was the least popular?
...... Kids Toons ......

How many children were involved in the survey? | 48 | children

How many more children preferred Pop Juniors to Kids Toons? | 4 | children

Which two channels had a total number of 25 votes?
...... Cartoon Kids and Pop Juniors ......

Explain how the results might have been different if adults rather than children were surveyed.
...... Answers may vary ......

What was the difference in numbers between the most popular and the least popular television channel? | 9 |

Many different forms of data display exist and whenever you see an example show it to your child. Discuss it and ask him/her questions such as "Is it obvious what it's about?", "Does it have a title?" and "Is the data clear or confusing?"

---

24 — ★ Addition and subtraction 3

The sum of two numbers is 75. One number is 18. What is the other number? **Note:** This problem can be solved in different ways.
| 57 |

$$75 - 18 = 57$$
or
$$18 + 2 = 20$$
$$20 + 50 = 70$$
$$70 + 5 = 75$$
$$2 + 50 + 5 = 57$$

Last month, Sebastian delivered parcels to four shops in Bond Street. He delivered 12 parcels to one shop, 37 to the next shop, 28 to the third and 31 to the final shop. How many parcels did Sebastian deliver altogether?
| 108 | parcels

For their last holiday, the Robinsons went on a long road trip. On the first day of their holiday, they drove 190 km. On the second day they drove 165 km and on the final day they drove 85 km. How many kilometres in total did the Robinsons travel?
| 440 km |

Amal put her building blocks into three piles according to their colours, which were red, blue and yellow. There were 20 blocks in the red pile and 35 blocks in the blue pile. If Amal has a total of 100 blocks, how many yellow blocks did she have?
| 45 | yellow blocks

Xavier challenged Liam to a computer game. Liam scored 200 points. However, Xavier beat Liam's score by 130 points. How many points did Xavier score?
| 330 | points

The difference between two numbers is 17. The larger number is 50. What is the smaller number?
| 33 |

Your child needs to know the different terms used to mean "add" and "subtract". "Add" terms include "combine", "join", "put together" and "altogether". "Subtract" terms include "take away", "decrease" and "less than".

---

25 — Addition and subtraction 4 ★

Forty-nine people auditioned for a dance company over two days. If 26 people were selected on the first day and four more on the second day, how many people were not chosen?
| 19 | people

$$26 + 4 = 30$$
$$\begin{array}{r} 49 \\ -\ 30 \\ \hline 19 \end{array}$$

When three numbers are added together, the total is 150. Two of the numbers are 20 and 35. What is the third number?
| 95 |

When two different numbers are added together, their total is 12. If one of the numbers is double the other, what are the two numbers?
| 4 | and | 8 |

The United Nations, or UN, has 193 member countries. Of these, 51 countries were original members of the organisation. How many member countries are not original members of the UN?
| 142 | countries

Four classes from Knightwood Primary School went on a school picnic. The number of children and helpers for each class were 37, 36, 29 and 38. What was the total number of children and helpers at the picnic?
| 140 | children and helpers

For a science fair, Beatrice made a working model of a drawbridge. The model was made up of 73 different pieces, of which 34 pieces were metal and the rest plastic. How many plastic pieces did Beatrice use in her model?
| 39 | plastic pieces

Your child should know that every sum, even simple ones, gives more information than he/she might think. For example, 4 + 7 = 11, so 11 – 7 = 4 and 11 – 4 = 7. This ability to "link" calculations is worth pointing out to him/her.

---

26 — ★ Multiplication and division 3

Daniel played a new game on his computer. He had three tries and achieved the same score each time. If Daniel had scored a total of 27 points, how many points did he score in each try?
| 9 | points

$$27 \div 3 = 9$$

Guests at Rupert's party were seated at tables of eight. If 56 guests attended the party, how many tables did Rupert need for his guests?
| 7 | tables

The fence panels Harriet bought for her garden are sold in packs of four. If Harriet used 36 panels, how many packs did she buy?
| 9 | packs

A decade is the same as 10 years. How many decades are the same as 110 years?
| 11 | decades

A number is multiplied by itself and the answer is then doubled. If the final number is 50, what was the original number?
| 5 |

Schoolchildren at Gilmore Academy took part in a cross-country race. They were divided into groups of nine. If there were seven groups in the race, how many children took part?
| 63 | children

Lillian made a large cube out of small cubes. Each edge of the large cube was four times the length of the edge of a small cube. How many small cubes were used to make the large cube?
| 64 | small cubes

By now, your child should be aware of the written methods of multiplication and division. He/she should also be familiar with the methods of combining mental calculations with written ones.

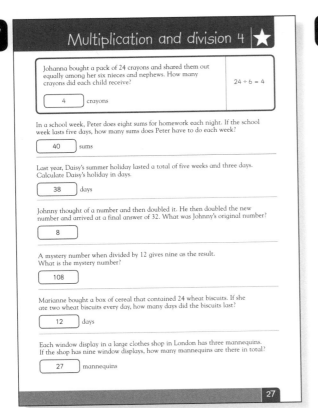

Multiplication and division 4 ★

Johanna bought a pack of 24 crayons and shared them out equally among her six nieces and nephews. How many crayons did each child receive?

$24 ÷ 6 = 4$

[4] crayons

In a school week, Peter does eight sums for homework each night. If the school week lasts five days, how many sums does Peter have to do each week?

[40] sums

Last year, Daisy's summer holiday lasted a total of five weeks and three days. Calculate Daisy's holiday in days.

[38] days

Johnny thought of a number and then doubled it. He then doubled the new number and arrived at a final answer of 32. What was Johnny's original number?

[8]

A mystery number when divided by 12 gives nine as the result. What is the mystery number?

[108]

Marianne bought a box of cereal that contained 24 wheat biscuits. If she ate two wheat biscuits every day, how many days did the biscuits last?

[12] days

Each window display in a large clothes shop in London has three mannequins. If the shop has nine window displays, how many mannequins are there in total?

[27] mannequins

Tell your child that each combination in a sum generates more information. For 4 x 5 = 20, the combinations generated are 5 x 4 = 20, 20 ÷ 4 = 5 and 20 ÷ 5 = 4. Ask your child to supply similar combinations for other sums.

★ General calculations 1

The perimeter of a rectangle is 26 cm and its width is 4 cm. Calculate its length.	Perimeter = (2 x length) + (2 x width) 2 x 4 taken away from 26 will give you twice the length. $26 - 8 = 18$ $18 ÷ 2 = 9$
[9 cm]	

At a shopping centre, Ava paid the £1.65 fee for parking with coins. She used the fewest number of coins to give the exact amount. What were they?

[£1] [50 p] [10 p] [5 p]

The perimeter of a rectangle is 18 cm. The shorter side of the rectangle is half the length of the longer side. What are the lengths of the sides?

[6 cm] and [3 cm]

A bowl contains 36 pieces of fruit. One-sixth of them are oranges. How many pieces of fruit in the bowl are not oranges?

[30] pieces of fruit

Out of 90 contestants in a talent show, 10% danced and the rest sang. How many contestants sang?

[81]

The distance between Wigan and Birch Green is 8.9 miles. What is the total distance travelled if you go from Wigan to Birch Green and then back again?

[17.8 miles]

In his wardrobe, Julian has ties and shirts in the ratio of 1:5. If Julian has a total of 18 ties and shirts, how many does he have of each?

[3] ties   [15] shirts

When your child comes across problems that require more than one operation, ask him to read them more than once to determine which operations are needed.

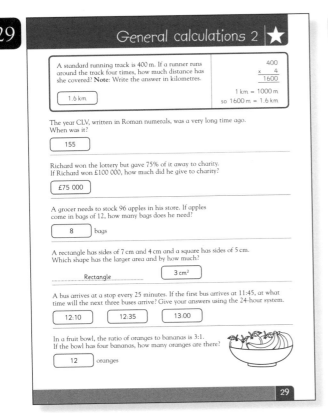

General calculations 2 ★

A standard running track is 400 m. If a runner runs around the track four times, how much distance has she covered? **Note**: Write the answer in kilometres.

```
   400
 x   4
  1600
```
1 km = 1000 m
so 1600 m = 1.6 km

[1.6 km]

The year CLV, written in Roman numerals, was a very long time ago. When was it?

[155]

Richard won the lottery but gave 75% of it away to charity. If Richard won £100 000, how much did he give to charity?

[£75 000]

A grocer needs to stock 96 apples in his store. If apples come in bags of 12, how many bags does he need?

[8] bags

A rectangle has sides of 7 cm and 4 cm and a square has sides of 5 cm. Which shape has the larger area and by how much?

Rectangle   [3 cm²]

A bus arrives at a stop every 25 minutes. If the first bus arrives at 11:45, at what time will the next three buses arrive? Give your answers using the 24-hour system.

[12:10] [12:35] [13:00]

In a fruit bowl, the ratio of oranges to bananas is 3:1. If the bowl has four bananas, how many oranges are there?

[12] oranges

Make sure your child understands which numbers and operation(s) are needed to solve each problem. Sometimes, the operations may not have simple terms, such as "add", so she will need to be very alert.

★ Harder problems 1

Cleo went to a shop to buy new trainers. She liked a pair that cost £87. However, she used a discount voucher and only had to pay £42.70. How much did Cleo save?

```
  87.00
- 42.70
  44.30
```

[£44.30]

Trinny follows the same exercise regime every day. She jogs 1.3 km at a steady pace every 15 minutes. What time does Trinny finish if she leaves home at 15:40 every day and jogs a total distance of 6.5 km? Give your answer using the 24-hour system.

[16:55]

What is the area of the shape on the right?

[39 cm²]

The cost of posting a parcel depends on its weight. If a parcel weighing 2 kg costs £2.80 to post, what will a parcel weighing 10 kg cost?

[£14]

Mila tiled her bathroom floor. For each green tile she used, she used five white tiles. If Mila used 30 tiles, how many of each colour did she use?

Green [5]   White [25]

The perimeter of a regular hexagon is 78 cm. What is the length of each side?

[13 cm]

Sean multiplied a number by itself and then halved it. The result was 24.5. Which number did Sean start with?

[7]

When your child completes a problem, check if the proper operations have been carried out. Also, check if the numbers have been written down properly. Finally, check the answer by doing a rough estimation.

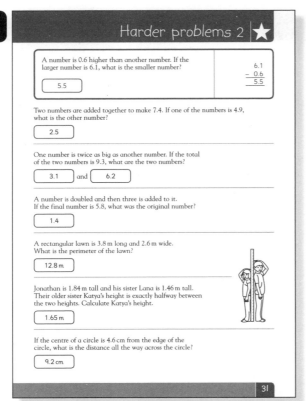

A number is 0.6 higher than another number. If the larger number is 6.1, what is the smaller number?

5.5

$$\begin{array}{r} 6.1 \\ -\ 0.6 \\ \hline 5.5 \end{array}$$

Two numbers are added together to make 7.4. If one of the numbers is 4.9, what is the other number?

2.5

One number is twice as big as another number. If the total of the two numbers is 9.3, what are the two numbers?

3.1 and 6.2

A number is doubled and then three is added to it. If the final number is 5.8, what was the original number?

1.4

A rectangular lawn is 3.8 m long and 2.6 m wide. What is the perimeter of the lawn?

12.8 m

Jonathan is 1.84 m tall and his sister Lana is 1.46 m tall. Their older sister Katya's height is exactly halfway between the two heights. Calculate Katya's height.

1.65 m

If the centre of a circle is 4.6 cm from the edge of the circle, what is the distance all the way across the circle?

9.2 cm

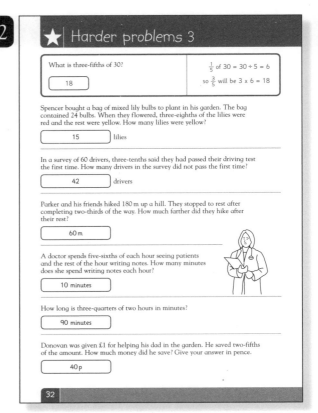

What is three-fifths of 30?

18

$\frac{1}{5}$ of 30 = 30 ÷ 5 = 6
so $\frac{3}{5}$ will be 3 x 6 = 18

Spencer bought a bag of mixed lily bulbs to plant in his garden. The bag contained 24 bulbs. When they flowered, three-eighths of the lilies were red and the rest were yellow. How many lilies were yellow?

15 lilies

In a survey of 60 drivers, three-tenths said they had passed their driving test the first time. How many drivers in the survey did not pass the first time?

42 drivers

Parker and his friends hiked 180 m up a hill. They stopped to rest after completing two-thirds of the way. How much farther did they hike after their rest?

60 m

A doctor spends five-sixths of each hour seeing patients and the rest of the hour writing notes. How many minutes does she spend writing notes each hour?

10 minutes

How long is three-quarters of two hours in minutes?

90 minutes

Donovan was given £1 for helping his dad in the garden. He saved two-fifths of the amount. How much money did he save? Give your answer in pence.

40 p

As the wording of questions becomes more complex, your child can lose sight of the decimal amounts involved. Ensure she/he reads the sums carefully and then writes down the numbers and operations involved.

By now, your child will be used to difficult fractions, such as $\frac{2}{3}$ or $\frac{4}{9}$. He/she can solve problems by finding the unitary value and then using multiplication. So $\frac{5}{6}$ of 18 involves finding $\frac{1}{6}$ of 18 and then multiplying the result by 5.